D1212703

MEMS & NANOTECHNOLOGY FOR **KIDS**

MARLENE BOURNE

Bourne Research LLC
Scottsdale, AZ

Cover by Nocturnal Graphic Design

ISBN-10: 0-9795505-6-4
ISBN-13: 978-0-9795505-6-0

Library of Congress Control Number: 2007905240

Published by Bourne Research LLC
8867 E. Mountain Spring Rd
Scottsdale, AZ 85255
www.bourneresearch.com

Printed in the United States of America

September 2007

First Edition

10 9 8 7 6 5 4 3 2 1

A special thank you to Clay (an 11 year-old "super scientist"),
and Brianna (an extraordinary 11 year-old), for their enthusiastic
feedback and suggestions.

Small is Cool!

Imagine a world where ants and butterflies are giants; an amazing world full of tiny machines and structures far smaller than the dot at the end of this sentence.

Some call the things in this extraordinary world micro-bots and nano-bots. Many think they're magical: some have the ability to become invisible, others are stronger than steel, and some might even save lives.

Is this true? Perhaps.

Are they real? Yes.

Photo courtesy of DENSO Corporation

In 1995, the Guinness Book of Records recognized DENSO Corporation for the world's smallest motor car. This 1/1000th replica of Toyota's 1936 Model AA Sedan had 24 individual parts—including a shell body, chassis, tires, wheels, axles, headlights, tail lights, bumpers, a spare tire and hubcaps. It reached a top speed of 10 cm/sec.

Small is Cool!

Welcome to the wonderful world of really small stuff. Things so tiny, you need special microscopes to even see them.

This book takes you into the micro- and nano-world to look at incredibly small sensors, structures and materials created by scientists and engineers all around the world.

You'll find out what these things are, how they work, what makes them so special and why they're being used in all sorts of products—from bikes to video games.

The "bracelet" on the ant's arm in the photo below is actually a tiny gear. Gears like this (only a lot bigger) are used to create motion or to change speed or direction. They're found everywhere; almost anything that is mechanical uses gears of some kind, such as bikes and clocks. Tiny gears like the one on the ant are found in things such as small pumps used to deliver medicine into the body.

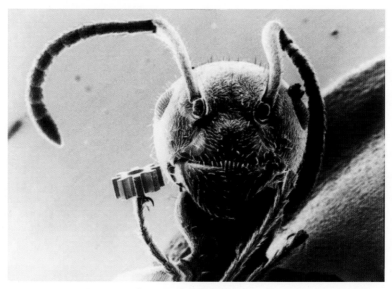

Ant with MEMS gear © Copyright 2007 Forschungszentrum Karlsruhe

How Small Is It?

All of the things discussed in this book are smaller than the diameter of a human hair. Go ahead—pull one out of your head and take a look. It's pretty tiny, isn't it? One human hair is about 80 micrometers in diameter.

What is a micrometer? You're probably more familiar with inches and millimeters. One inch equals 25.4 millimeters. There are 1,000 micrometers in one millimeter.

The strings that are part of an electric guitar range in size from one millimeter to .62 millimeters (or 620 micrometers). So, about seven or eight human hairs placed side-by-side would equal the thinnest guitar string.

One of the smallest guitars ever made is just ten micrometers long—about eight placed end-to-end would fit across the width of a single hair. Each string on that guitar is 50 nanometers wide. In this case, you could place nearly 100,000 of these tiny strings side-by-side on one human hair!

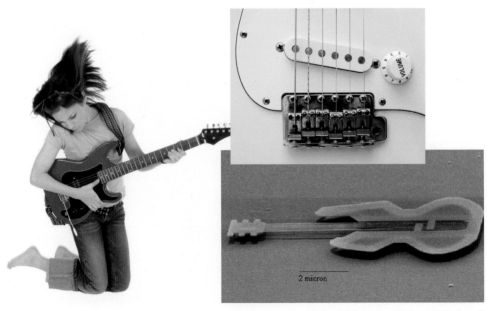

Photo courtesy of Harold Craighead, Cornell University

Micro-Scale

The reddish-brown ants you might see in your house or at the park are just two to three millimeters long, or about 2,000 to 3,000 micrometers.

As we just discussed, a human hair is about 80 micrometers in diameter; that's approximately the same thickness as a piece of notebook paper.

Pollen is the powdery stuff on flowers. In the picture to the left, it's the purple grains stuck to the bee as it crawls across the flower. Pollen grains range in size from 25 to 50 micrometers. *Billions* of pollen grains will fit in one teaspoon!

Micro-Scale

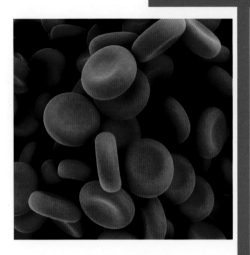

Blood is made up of red blood cells (which give blood its color) and white blood cells. A single red blood cell is about seven micrometers in diameter.

One micrometer equals 1,000 nanometers.

Some bacteria are good, but some can make you sick or even cause infections. Did you know that your feet get smelly when sweat from your feet mixes with bacteria on your skin? In terms of size, bacteria are typically one to three micrometers in diameter.

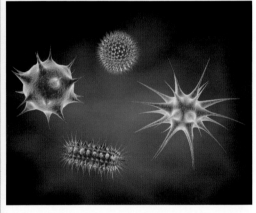

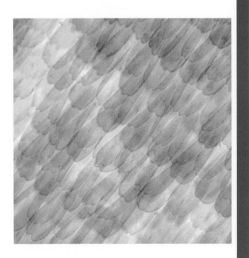

If you looked under a microscope, you'll discover that the wings of some butterflies are actually made up of scales—sort of like the shingles on a roof. Each of these scales is about 90 nanometers thick. One thousand of these scales stacked on top of each other would fit across a single human hair.

Nano-Scale

Viruses make us sick—when you get a cold it's because of a virus. The virus that causes the common cold is about 20 nanometers in diameter. Isn't it interesting to see how "fuzzy" the surface of a virus looks? How small do you think those little hairs are?

A cluster of atoms (see description below) is what makes a molecule. The photo to the left illustrates how water is made of two hydrogen atoms (the black dots) and one oxygen atom (the red dots)—they're illustrated in red and black only so you can see them. The width of a single water molecule is about one nanometer.

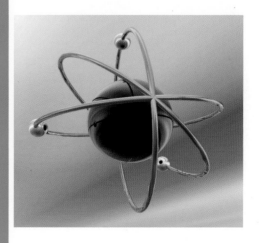

Atoms are the basic building block of chemistry and are just one-third of a nanometer wide. Made of electrons, protons and neutrons, an atom that doesn't have the same number of electrons and protons is an ion.

The Micro-World

Now that we have an idea of how small things are in the micro-world, let's take a look at some of the products made at this size. This is where we'll find "micro-bots" or things called MEMS (Micro-Electro-Mechanical Systems).

MEMS are tiny structures that combine both a mechanical component and electronic circuits on a single semiconductor chip. What can MEMS do that semiconductors can't? Microprocessors and micro-controllers are the brains of electronic products. MEMS are the eyes, ears, nose, arms and legs that help the brain know what's going on and decide what it should do.

MEMS can do things like sense motion and pressure, move light and liquid, and even "smell" chemicals. The dimensions of MEMS devices are micro-scale, falling within the range of 1 to 100 micrometers, or somewhere between the size of a human hair and a single bacteria.

There are all sorts of MEMS. The most common are accelerometers, gyro sensors, pressure sensors, nozzles, optical MEMS and lab-on-a-chip. The photos below are of pieces of a complex lock smaller than an ant; the tiny teeth of the MEMS gears are just a few micrometers wide!

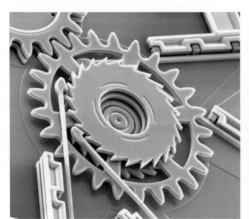

Photos courtesy of Sandia National Laboratories,
SUMMiT™ Technologies, www.mems.sandia.gov

Accelerometer

An accelerometer measures linear or two-dimensional movement along one of three axes: X, Y and Z.

- The X-axis is like the green elevator door; it can move left or right.

- The Y-axis is the same as if you take a step forward or backward through the door.

- The Z-axis is like rolling the window of a car up and down.

The motion accelerometers measure can range from subtle, like the vibration generated by a running motor, to the obvious, such as the swing of your arm; or even the shock generated if you walked into a wall.

Accelerometers can also measure tilt. When you open the door of an oven, it tilts outward. See how the pan of cookies tilts while placing it in the oven? Both the X and Z axis can measure those angles of tilt.

Accelerometer

More than 200 million accelerometers are sold each year—most of them for use in cars. They're the sensors that detect if a car hits something and determines if the airbags should open.

Accelerometers are also found in some cell phones. They can count the number of steps you take (like a pedometer), or know if the phone is being held vertically or horizontally (and re-adjust the screen's position).

Accelerometers are also used to teach people how to golf better. Attached to the club itself, a special vest you wear, or even a hat, the sensors monitor how you swing the club. It then provides feedback so you can learn to swing more efficiently.

One of the most exciting uses of these sensors is in the new Nintendo Wii™ gaming system. MEMS accelerometers are what make the controller work the way it does. Now you can do things like play baseball in your living room! How? As the images below illustrate, your character (in the red shirt in the upper left) is at bat. You hold the controller like a baseball bat and swing at the ball as the pitcher throws it—and maybe hit a home run!

Images courtesy of Nintendo

Gyro Sensor

A gyro sensor measures three kinds of rotational movement: yaw (side to side), pitch (up and down) and roll. If you've been on an airplane when there is turbulence, then you've experienced yaw, pitch and roll first-hand.

When the plane moves from side to side (like twisting in your seat to talk to someone on your left or right), that's yaw. When the nose of the plane tilts up or down (and you lean forward or backward), that's pitch. And as the plane makes a steep turn to the left or to the right, that's roll.

The combination of an accelerometer with a gyro sensor creates what is called an Inertial Measurement Unit (IMU). In this case, the sensor is able to monitor all types of linear *and* rotational movement independently of each other: left and right, forward and backward, up and down, yaw, pitch and roll. An IMU is what makes the Segway® Personal Transporter work. Lean to the right and you will turn right; stand up straight and you will stop. It mimics human balance. Except, rather than using your legs to walk, you glide on two wheels.

Photo courtesy of Segway Inc.

Pressure Sensor

Pressure sensors measure the pressure of gas, liquid, vapor and even dust. This is generally done by monitoring how much a thin membrane moves while under pressure. If there's no pressure, it doesn't move at all. Under high pressure, the membrane will move quite a bit.

Take a tissue or paper towel and place it tightly over the top of a glass. Now, lightly place your finger on it. Do you see it move? That's a little bit like the motion a membrane experiences in the presence of low pressure. The more pressure you apply, the more the tissue bends. This is what can occur under high pressure.

Pressure sensors are used in a lot of industrial machinery to control the pressure of liquids, like the water used to clean and manufacture food. These sensors are also used to monitor air pressure in the tanks of SCUBA divers, as well as in the watches they use to know their depth. The photo below shows a sensor that is implanted right into the heart to monitor pressure after the insertion of a stent. A stent is a tiny metal scaffold that is placed inside an artery to help keep it open.

Photo courtesy of Georgia Tech/Gary Meek

Nozzles

The first ink jet cartridges had just 12 nozzles and could print 1,000 drops in one second. Today's printheads have hundreds of nozzles and can print at rates of 18 million drops per second, with droplet sizes as small as one nanometer. MEMS ink jet cartridges use a technology called thermal bubble. Ink fills a cavity, which is then heated, creating bubbles (hence the name, thermal bubble). These bubbles of ink are then propelled out of the nozzle onto the paper. The empty cavity fills with ink and the process repeats itself thousands of times per *second*.

Illustrations courtesy of STMicroelectronics

Do you know how cakes that have a photo on them are made? An ink jet printer filled with edible ink "prints" the photo onto super-thin "paper" made from rice or starch, which is then placed on the cake. As the paper dissolves, the photo becomes part of the frosting. One of the newest ink jet printers, from FUJIFILM Dimatix, is used to print colorful, edible patterns, images and even trivia onto food like chocolates and potato chips!

To the right is a close-up of ink as it is being propelled out of ink jet nozzles.

The photo "Tails of the Nozzle Bank" was taken by Dr. Steve Hoath of the Department of Engineering at the University of Cambridge (www.eng.cam.ac.uk). It was part of a photo competition sponsored by Epson (www.epson.co.uk).

Optical MEMS

The brief flash of sunlight off a reflective surface is something that you can't help but notice. A signal mirror (a small, handheld mirror) is an important piece of survival gear. Reflecting the sun to create a flash of light is far more efficient, and noticeable, than simply waving your arms.

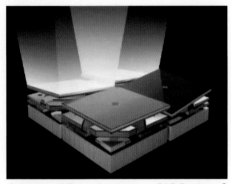

Courtesy of Texas Instruments DLP Products®

An optical MEMS device is a tiny little mirror that reflects or moves light. The DLP® (Digital Light Processor) from Texas Instruments contains nearly 2.2 *million* of these little moving mirrors on a chip less than one-inch square—or slightly smaller than a pecan! They're used to create the picture of your television and project the movies you see in theaters.

Optical MEMS are also used to create "wearable" displays. They look just like sunglasses, but when you wear them, you can watch movies or videos just like you're sitting in front of a big TV!

Photo courtesy of myvu

© 2006 Luminetx Technologies Corporation

The VeinViewer by Luminetx™ is really unique. It uses infrared light and an optical MEMS chip to create an image of the veins just under the skin. Now technicians know exactly where to insert needles so there's no more guessing!

Lab-on-a-Chip

Lab-on-a-chip devices are unique sensors made of tiny channels, pumps and valves etched into plastic, glass or silicon. To detect chemicals, they mix and control extremely small amounts of fluid like blood or water.

That's not as easy as it sounds. This is because liquid has completely different properties at the micro scale. Water in a drinking glass moves freely and can be splashed about. But in a lab-on-a-chip device, water takes on a property called "laminar flow." That means it moves really slowly and smoothly, like lava oozing out from a volcano, or pouring thick syrup.

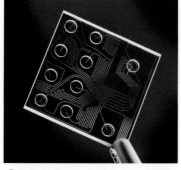

© Agilent Technologies, Inc. 2007

Hospitals use lab-on-a-chip in emergency rooms for point-of-care diagnostics (POC). In the past, doctors sometimes had to wait several hours for the results of blood tests. Now, using just one drop of blood, doctors can start to figure out what might be wrong—in as little as two minutes!

Most of these chips are used to detect all sorts of chemicals in the blood, such as certain gases, glucose and electrolytes. A few can even detect if someone is having a heart attack! During a heart attack, three different proteins are released into the blood. Special chips are able to detect these specific proteins.

The Nano-World

Nanotechnology is all about the ability to produce materials and structures that are 1 to 100 nanometers in size; some call these things nano-bots.

Why do scientists and companies want to do this? As you move from the micro- to the nano-world, the physical, chemical and biological properties of a material changes. How a material works and the properties it exhibits as a micro-particle, is often very different from how a material works and the properties it exhibits as a nanoparticle.

As we have already discussed (and seen), both microparticles and nano-particles are extremely small. So, what's the difference between the two?

Let's pretend that a particle 10 micrometers in diameter is the size of an elephant, and that a particle 10 nanometers in diameter is the size of a mouse. As you can see in the picture to the right, there's a big size difference.

One of the most important properties of a nanoscale material is surface area. Let's say you have two sugar cubes. Now, crush one. The big sugar cube is like the elephant. All of the little crystals from the crushed sugar cube are like the mouse. You have an equal amount of sugar, but the crushed sugar has more surface area.

Because of their tiny size and increased surface area, you can do a lot more with the smaller particles. A big advantage is you will use a lot less. And, you could coat a larger particle with the smaller particles. So, what are some of their other special properties?

Nanoparticles

Nanoparticles can make products that are softer and smoother, because the particles are so small. Let's use sand and garden soil as an example, and pretend that the particles of sand are microscale and the particles of garden soil are nanoscale. This is a good illustration, because sand you find at the beach is typically much coarser than the soil in a garden. If you mix sand with water, the mud feels rough because the particles are fairly large. The garden soil particles are much smaller; so when you mix those with water, the mixture is softer and smoother than the mixture made with sand.

Nanoparticles also blend together better. Take a glass of water and add some oil. The oil floats on top, right? If you shake it, the oil will mix with the water, but not very well. But if the oil particles were nanoscale, they would not only mix with the water much easier, but they will stay mixed together for a longer period of time.

 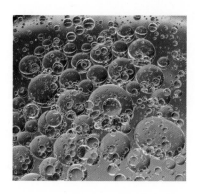

Nanoparticles

Some materials become transparent, or clear, at the nanoscale. The best example here is sunscreen. In the past, many lifeguards at the beach or pool had a white nose. This is because they used zinc oxide to protect their noses from getting burned from the sun. At the nansocale, zinc oxide is clear—so seeing white noses at the beach is now a thing of the past.

But nanoparticles aren't necessarily a modern invention; nor are they always man-made. Not only have nanoparticles been used in products for centuries, but some nanoparticles occur naturally. We didn't know this until recently, because the special equipment that allows scientists to study things at the nanoscale really wasn't available until the 1990s.

The ancient Egyptians were among the first to use nanoparticles—in cosmetics. The main ingredient in the distinctive black eyeliner they used around their eyes is called carbon black (although they called it lamp black). The particles of the fluffy, black soot created when burning candles or oil lamps are actually nanoscale. Carbon black was not only an ingredient in eyeliner, but the Chinese also used it to make ink. Today, carbon black is a major ingredient in tires and the ink used to print newspapers.

Nanoparticles

Two of the materials we just discussed, zinc oxide and carbon black, are very popular nanoparticles. But some of the most widely used nanoparticles are iron oxides. There are sixteen different iron oxides; most are found in pigments, which are used to create color. This ranges from the deep blue glazes used to decorate pottery and floor tiles, to paint. Nanoparticles of iron oxides are already used to create the paint used on cars, and all sorts of things with a painted finish, like home appliances. Even cosmetics use nanoparticles of iron oxides to give color to things like nail polish, lipstick and eye shadow.

All sorts of materials can be made at the nanoscale. Some of the most unique include aerogels, carbon nanotubes, fullerenes, buckyballs, dendrimers, nanoclay and nanofibers. Let's take a look at what they are, what they do and how they are being used in all kinds of products.

Aerogels

One of the lightest materials in the world, aerogels are three times lighter than air, and 4,000 times stronger than their own weight. They are sometimes called frozen smoke, because that is sort of what they look like. Structurally, aerogels are similar to sponges, but feel like Styrofoam.

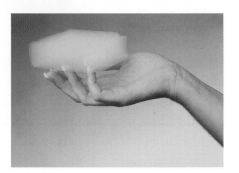

Photo courtesy NASA/JPL

Although they don't look like much, aerogels have remarkable insulating properties; this is because they are made of nanoscale pockets of air. This incredible amount of surface area allows aerogels to block all three types of heat transfer: convection (despite being mostly air, air can't circulate through the material), conduction (aerogels don't conduct heat well), and radiation (aerogels absorb infrared heat).

Aerogels were first used to insulate the spacesuits worn by astronauts, as well as protect the electronics of the Mars Pathfinder on its mission to the red planet in the 1990s. Today, aerogels can be found as an insulation material in windows, and home appliances like refrigerators. They are also used in shoes to help keep your feet from getting cold.

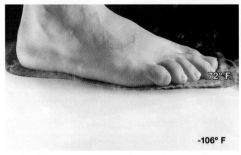

72° F.

-106° F

Photo courtesy of Aspen Aerogels Inc.

The thin, orange footbed (or insole) in the photo to the left, which is made with Aspen Aerogels™, can protect a bare foot from the cold of dry ice—which has a temperature of minus 106° F!—while the foot stays a warm 72° F.

Carbon Nanotubes

Carbon nanotubes (CNT) are a cylindrical, tube-like arrangement of carbon atoms that are about one nanometer in diameter. If you unrolled one, you would see a honeycomb-like structure.

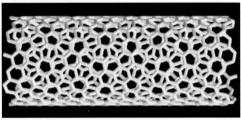

Photo courtesy of Jian-Min Zuo,
University of Illinois Urbana-Champaign

Next time you are at the hardware store, go the fencing section and take a look at the chicken wire. It also has holes that are hexagonal in shape (like a honeycomb). If you cut a section and roll it into a tube, you will have a structure that looks like a carbon nanotube— except a lot bigger.

Carbon nanotubes are incredibly strong—100 times stronger than steel— and very light. In fact, carbon nanotubes are 1/6th the weight of steel. They are also flexible, and can conduct electricity as well as copper.

Right now, carbon nanotubes are mostly used as a composite material. That means they're mixed together with a polymer (another word for plastic) to create a material that is both lighter and stronger than regular plastic.

In 2005, BMC introduced a new bike whose frame was made with a carbon nanotube composite—the Phonak team raced on these bikes in the 2005 Tour de France. Carbon nanotubes are also found in baseball and softball bats, hockey sticks, tennis racquets and more.

Dendrimers

Dendrimers are three-dimensional, star-shaped molecules that can be as small as three or four nanometers in diameter. They look a little bit like a snowflake, don't they? Dendrimers dissolve quickly in water and have low viscosity. This means they flow easily (like milk)—unlike mashed potatoes, which have a higher viscosity and don't flow easily.

Photo courtesy Cambridge Display Technology

Dendrimers also have low compressibility. This means they won't decrease very much under pressure. Like the boy in the photo to the left, a tile floor won't bend when you sit on it. So, this floor has low compressibility. But if you sit in a soft, squishy pillow, like the cat, you sink in; this pillow has high compressibility.

Dendrimers are used to make materials more water resistant and stick better to surfaces they are applied to. Dendrimers also help liquid materials dry faster. Because of these properties, it makes sense that they are being used in new ink jet inks.

Where else are they found? Some companies are using dendrimers to improve the delivery of drugs into the body. Others are using them to create new displays for televisions and various consumer electronics.

Fullerenes

Fullerenes (also called buckyballs) are molecular clusters of carbon, which look a lot like a soccer ball. Fullerenes are extremely hard, can withstand high temperature and pressure (they spring back to shape when compressed) and they also bounce!

Photo courtesy of Lawrence Berkeley National Laboratory

The fact that fullerenes are hollow is one of their most unique properties. Because of this, researchers are very interested in their potential use in all sorts of medical applications, such as drug delivery, because they can be "filled" with various materials.

200 nm

Photo Courtesy of Dan Luo, Cornell University

One of the first applications of fullerenes was a coating for bowling balls. This made the balls resistant to chipping and cracking; it also made them glide better on their way down the lane into the pins—or the gutter.

Nanoclay

A lot of companies are very excited about nanoclay—or, nanoparticles of clay. Like zinc oxide, clay becomes transparent at the nanoscale. One area where this is very useful is in composite materials, which is another way of describing what plastics are.

A composite is made of two components: a matrix, which is basically the base material, and a filler of some kind. The filler is mixed into the matrix to make it stronger. A good example is water (the matrix) and instant potato flakes (the filler). The dried flakes, when added to the water, make a material (mashed potatoes), that's a lot denser (or stronger) than just water alone. Adjusting the ratio of matrix and filler can change the consistency, and properties, of the end product.

With current plastics, the filler is generally talc (what baby powder is made of) or glass—but they can make plastic cloudy. Because nanoclay is transparent, it doesn't affect the color. Plus, because there's more surface area, less is needed, so the plastic remains flexible. In addition, the increased surface area acts as a barrier, so air won't move in and out of the plastic. This is very important to companies who produce food—just think of all the plastics used to package food, from bottles to plastic wrap.

Did you know that some tennis balls have pressurized air inside? That's what helps them bounce. But as the air leaks out, they stop bouncing. A few years ago, the inside of some tennis balls were coated with nanoclay. As a result, the air didn't leak out as fast, so they bounced longer.

Nanofibers

Nanofibers—which are essentially fibers at the nanoscale—are created by a process called electrospinning.

The process works like this: a needle is filled with a liquid polymer (plastic), electricity is applied to pull out the material in a continuous stream and then it's whipped around really fast so that the stream of material can be stretched into nanometer dimensions. The end result is a web of tiny fibers. The process is similar to creating cotton candy, but at the nanoscale.

The large, brownish object in the photo to the right is a human hair. You can see that hairs have an outer coating made of scales which overlap each other and look a little bit like the shingles on a roof. The tiny white threads are nanofibers!

Photo courtesy of eSpin Technologies

Nanofibers are spun for use as both textiles (called woven materials because thread or yarn is woven together) and membranes (called non-woven materials because the threads are just pressed together). Membranes are used to filter things like water and air—like the air filter to the left, which is used in cars.

Nanowhiskers

A really unique nanomaterial is a nanowhisker. These are being used to make clothes resistant to stains and create self-cleaning windows!

The concept is based on the leaves of the lotus flower, which scientists discovered are self-cleaning. This isn't because the leaves are extremely smooth; instead, they are covered with naturally-occurring nanostructures that repel water. In fact, water droplets on such a surface retain an almost perfectly round shape. As the water droplet rolls off the leaf, it picks up dust and dirt particles along the way. So, when it rains, instead of water spots and bits of dirt being left behind, the leaves are clean.

The two photos below show the flat, irregular shape of water droplets on a regular leaf (or how water looks on a typical window), versus the almost perfectly round shape on a lotus leaf. Now, instead of window washers having to dangle from ropes to clean the windows of tall buildings, windows with this special coating will clean themselves whenever it rains.

Nanowhiskers

A company called Nano-Tex uses nano-whiskers to make clothes resistant to spills and stains. The technology works sort of like a peach. Think about that for a moment. Peaches have a very light layer of fuzz that you can barely see. But if you sprinkle water on one, it will typically just bead up and roll right off.

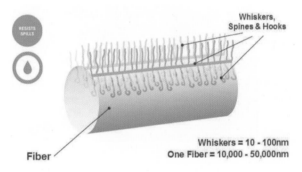

Illustration courtesy of Nano-Tex, Inc.

Tiny little nanowhiskers are attached to each of the fibers that are woven together to make fabric. How Nano-Tex does this is a secret, but one of the best qualities of this technology is that it doesn't make fabric stiff.

While most of the clothes that have this spill-resistant property are for adults (like pants, shirts and ties), wouldn't it be great for kids too? After all, how many times have you accidentally dropped food on your clothes? And wouldn't it be nice to not worry about getting into trouble if you accidentally spilled soda on the couch? A lot of companies that make fabrics now use this technology—not only for clothes, but for furniture as well.

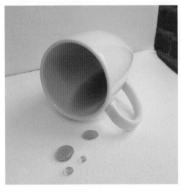

Photo courtesy of Nano-Tex, Inc.

27

More MEMS Things

Yes, this is a real fly, and yes, it's really wearing tiny MEMS glasses!

Photo courtesy of Micreon GmbH

The MEMS reed sensors to the right help to switch electric current on and off.

Photo courtesy of MEDER Electronic

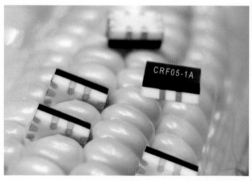

To the left is another kind of MEMS reed sensor; in this case, it is about the same size as a kernel of corn.

Photo courtesy of MEDER Electronic

Tiny little gears, like those to the right, are used in equally small pumps to dispense precise amounts of fluid.

Photo courtesy of HNP Mikrosysteme GmbH

More Nano Things

Pink-colored nanofibers are what give the rock rose quartz its color.

Photo courtesy of Prof. George Rossman and Julia Goreva, Caltech

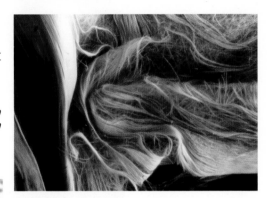

The "nanowire forest" to the left is made from zinc oxide.

Photo courtesy of Oak Ridge National Laboratory (Dr. Zhenwei Pan)

A close-up of individual particles of nano-scale powdered zinc oxide.

Photo courtesy of Prof. Witold Lojkowski, Tom Strachowski and Adam Presz, Unipress

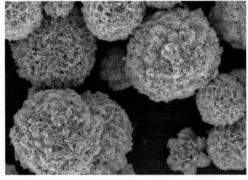

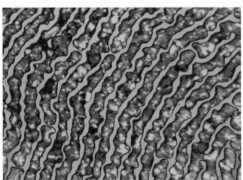

To the left are silver nanowires that have "self-assembled" themselves into neat rows.

Photo courtesy of Ward Lopes and Heinrich Jaeger, University of Chicago

About the Author

Hollye Schumacher Photography

Marlene Bourne, President & Principal Analyst of Bourne Research, is internationally recognized as one of the leading experts on MEMS and nanotechnology. With more than a decade of expertise as an industry analyst, she spends much of her time identifying technology, product and market trends to help companies be more competitive and grow their businesses.

Miss Bourne provides her opinions about emerging technologies to many business publications, including *Business 2.0*, *BusinessWeek*, *The Economist*, *Forbes*, *Investor's Business Daily*, *Los Angeles Times Magazine*, the *New York Times* and the *Wall Street Journal*.

She also produces and hosts a weekly podcast called *The Bourne Report*, and is the author of two books: *A Consumer's Guide to MEMS & Nanotechnology* and *MEMS & Nanotechnology for Kids*.

Miss Bourne holds a Bachelor of Science in Business from the University of Wisconsin—Stout and a Master of Arts in International Business and International Economics from the American University in Washington, DC.